THIS ACTIVITY BOOK BELONGS
TO LITTLE EXPLORER

_____

I'm Juan Carlos from Peru!

IT'S QUIZ TIME

1. What is Machu Picchu?

A. The phrase Peruvians use when they have too much food

B. The famous Incan citadel in the Andes mountains

2. Who were the *chasquis*?

A. Super fast runners and the messengers of the Incan Empire

B. The dancers of the Incan Empire

3. What are *caballitos de Totora*?

A. Plywood planes used by sailors in Huanchaco in Peru

B. Reed boats used by fishermen in Huanchaco in Peru

CAPITAL CITY:_ _ _ _

A   L

M   I

A salty ice challenge

The salt mines of Mara in Peru are known for their salt production. Salt has a pretty cool property. When you put salt on ice, it melts it, and then helps it refreeze! Let's try it.

WHAT YOU NEED: • water • salt • ice cube containers • tray • food coloring (or watercolors)

BUDDIFUL TIP: This is a messy experiment, so make sure to wear an apron or use an old shirt. Try it in the kitchen or outside!

1. Put water in a container and let it freeze. You can use an ice cube container or one with bigger holes.
2. Once frozen, empty the frozen pieces onto a tray.
3. Sprinkle (quite a lot!) of salt on top of each ice piece.
4. Add coloring to the surface.
5. The coloring will not color the ice, but it will help you trace the melting pattern. You'll notice that the salt melts the ice quite quickly and cracks will start appearing. You'll be able to see colorful channels, holes and tunnels in the ice.

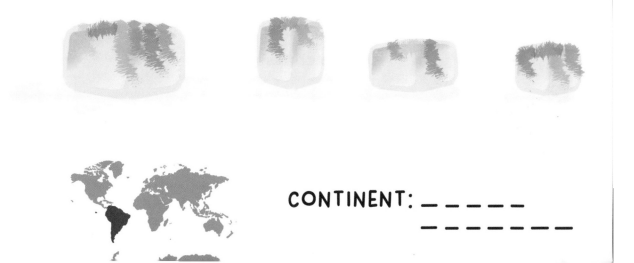

CONTINENT: _ _ _ _ _ _
_ _ _ _ _ _ _

I'm Athena from Greece!

IT'S QUIZ TIME

1. How many islands belong to Greece?
A. Around 6,000
B. 6

2. What is the name of the temple on the hill of the Acropolis in Athens?
A. The Aegean
B. The Parthenon

3. Which is the national cheese of Greece?
A. Edam cheese
B. Feta cheese

CAPITAL CITY:_ _ _ _ _ _

T A H
N S E

Crossword myths

* The Greek Gods and Goddesses lived on ....
1. Apollo is known as the God of .....
2. The number of the main Greek gods and goddesses is ......
3. Aphrodite, Goddess of Beauty and Love, was born out of .... from the sea.
4. The collection of myths and tales told by the Ancient Greeks is known as ....
5. The God of the Sky is ....

CONTINENT:_ _ _ _ _ _

I'm Ana from Brazil!

IT'S QUIZ TIME

1. Brazil shares a border with all
South American countries except two.
Which ones?
A. Chile and Mars
B. Chile and Ecuador

2. What are *blocos*?
A. Street parties that happen during the Rio carnival,
which is the biggest carnival in the world
B. A nickname Brazilians give to people
who are great at football

3. What is another name given
to the Amazon Rainforest?
A. The Lungs of the Earth
B. The Heart of the Earth

CAPITAL CITY: _ _ _ _ _ _ _ _

A L I
   A B
I S R

The Amazon rainforest

Tropical rainforests like the Amazon have four layers.
Match the animals below with the layers they live in.
Write their names or draw them!

FROGS   SLOTHS   TOUCANS   BIRDS   INSECTS   MONKEYS

BUTTERFLIES   JAGUARS   SNAKES   IGUANAS   ANT-EATERS

THE EMERGENT LAYER

is the top layer, with gigantic trees exposed
to lots of sunlight and strong winds.

THE CANOPY LAYER

is densely populated with all kinds
of trees. 90% of organisms live here.

THE UNDERSTORY LAYER

has young tress and plants
that survive with little sunlight.

THE FOREST FLOOR LAYER

contains fallen leaves, seeds and
fruits. Only 2% of sunlight reaches it.

CONTINENT: _ _ _ _ _

_ _ _ _ _ _ _

I'm Ife from Nigeria!

IT'S QUIZ TIME

1. Nigeria is a country with many ethnic groups. Some are ...

A. The Ojojo Omo People, the Yoruba People and the Hausa People

B. The Hausa People, the Yoruba People and the Igbo People

2. What is *jollof* rice?

A. An expression that means "everything is nice"

B. A famous type of rice that people cook in Nigeria

3. What is *ayo ayo*?

A. A traditional Nigerian game

B. The word Nigerians use to call their baby sister or brother

CAPITAL CITY: _ _ _ _ _

A
B J
A U

Kindness challenges

In Nigeria, people value community dearly and everyone helps around the house. Isn't that the nicest thing? You, too, can help. Start by completing the kindness challenges below.

DAY 1: THE EARLY MORNING CHALLENGE

Make your bed and the bed of everyone else in the house. They'll be super happy and surprised.

DAY 2: THE LAUNDRY DAY CHALLENGE

Help fold the laundry and match all the socks together— roll them up to make little sock-balls. Mismatch two pairs for some fun, mischievous days ahead.

DAY 3: THE ROLLY POLLY CHALLENGE

Change the toilet paper when it's done. But don't just throw the empty roll away. You can dress it up, color it and turn it into a little monster. BOO!

CONTINENT: _ _ _ _ _ _

I'm Rutger from the Netherlands!

IT'S QUIZ TIME

1. Which of these is an iconic symbol
of the Netherlands?
A. Windmills
B. Waterfalls

2. What is Friesland?
A. A province in the Netherlands
B. The way Dutch refer to the Netherlands
during winter

3. What is a *stroopwafel*?
A. The waffle that smurfs eat
B. Two thin wafer cookies
with a caramel filling

CAPITAL CITY:_____

R T A M M
A
D S E

A tulipful pattern

Every line of tulips follows a different color pattern.
Continue the patterns by drawing the missing tulips
with the correct colors.

CONTINENT: _ _ _ _ _ _ _

I'm Sām from Iran!

IT'S QUIZ TIME

1. Iran is famous for its ...
   A. Persian carpets
   B. Flowers and butterflies

2. On *Shab-e Yalda*, Iranians stay up all night and celebrate with friends, poetry and snacks. What is it?
   A. The longest night of the year, also known as the winter solstice
   B. The Iranian New Year, also known as *Nowruz*

3. What is the *Shahnameh*?
   A. A book with a very long poem of myths and stories from the past that has influenced Iran's culture
   B. A book with the name and address of every Iranian that ever lived

CAPITAL CITY: _ _ _ _ _ _ _

T A H
N R E

Sprouts 101

In Iran, *sabzeh*—sprouts—symbolize the beginning of life.
Grow your own *sabzeh* with lentils.

WHAT YOU NEED: • lentil seeds • bowl • plate • paper towel

DAY 1-3
- Place some lentil seeds in a bowl.
- Add water and let them soak, changing the water every day.

DAY 5-8
- The sprouts should begin to grow. Keep sprinkling them with water every day, but make sure not to drench the plate with water.

DAY 3-5
- After soaking the seeds, place them on a plate. You'll notice white sprouts starting to come out.
- Use a moist paper towel to cover the seeds.
- Sprinkle the seeds with water once a day.

DAY 8-14
- Place the plate on a windowsill so that they can see the sunlight. When the sprouts grow to ½ inch, remove the moist towel.
- Continue sprinkling them with water every day.
- The sprouts will grow and turn into a dark green.

DAY 14
- By now, your sprouts should be ready!

CONTINENT: _ _ _ _

I'm Zola from South Africa!

IT'S QUIZ TIME

1. What is South Africa known as?
   - A. The Faraway Nation
   - B. The Rainbow Nation

2. How many official languages does South Africa have?
   - A. 1
   - B. 12

3. What is a *braai*?
   - A. It's South Africa's special barbecue
   - B. It's South Africa's national celebration

CAPITAL CITY (1 OF 3): _ _ _ _   _ _ _ _

A P O
T N
C E W

Wilderness word trail

Kruger National Park in South Africa is one of Africa's largest natural reserves. It's known for its great variety of animals and untouched wilderness! Lizzy, the lazy lioness, wants to take a nap. In order to protect the animals while sleeping, she hid twelve of them inside the wilderness word trail below. Can you find them?

GAZELLE   BUFFALO   WILDEBEEST   ELEPHANT
ZEBRA   RHINO   IMPALA   ANTELOPE
LEOPARD   SQUIRREL   HYENA   GIRAFFE

```
L G A Z L L E I R K F
E I G A Z E L L E O I
L R I A N T E L O P E
E A Z I I M P A L A I
O F E B U P H Y E N A
P F B U F F A L O R E
A E R H I I N O I H I
R I A I Q Z T I T I R
D S Q U I R R E L N N
I Z F R O I E T I O I
W I L D E B E E S T O
```

CONTINENT: _ _ _ _ _ _

SOUTH AFRICA

I'm Koji from Japan!

IT'S QUIZ TIME

1. Which of these is one of Japan's most famous dishes?

    A. Fetuccine

    B. Sushi

2. Japan's name, which is pronounced as "Nippon", means …

A. The Sun's origin, because it's one of the first countries to see the rising sun every morning

B. The Moon's origin, because it's one of the first countries to see the moon every night

3. What is a *haiku*?

A. A Japanese poem of three lines and seventeen syllables

B. The sword of a *samurai*, who is a Japanese warrior

CAPITAL CITY: _ _ _ _ _   O y T

                                      K O

Origami secrets

Origami making is the Japanese art of folding a square piece of paper into different shapes and designs. Use a piece of paper to make a corner bookmark and decorate it in any way you like!

STEP 1
Take a square piece of paper.

STEP 2
Fold it in two.

STEP 3
Fold the left corner to the center.

STEP 4
Fold the right corner to the center.

STEP 5
Open up the triangle.

STEP 6
Fold the top flap of the center to the bottom to form a pocket.

STEP 7
Take the left corner and tuck it in the pocket. Take the right corner and tuck it in the pocket.

STEP 8
Decorate it and make it come to life! TA-DA!

CONTINENT:_ _ _ _

I'm Kwame from Ghana!

IT'S QUIZ TIME

1. In Ghana, your name sometimes indicates ...
A. The color of your eyes
B. The day you were born on

2. What is *kente*?
A. A Ghanaian textile made of colorful strips of silk and cotton
B. A famous Ghanaian story about Anansi the spider

3. Some of Ghana's ethnic groups are ...
A. The Akan, the Ewe and the Dagomba People
B. The Sotho, the Pedii and the Xhosa People

CAPITAL CITY:_ _ _ _ _

C A R
A C

Pi-lo-lo fun

In rural parts of Ghana children love to play *pilolo*,
a game of outdoor, simple fun. Are you ready?
Put on your sneakers and let's go!

1. Choose an object—sticks, coins, balls—and gather a number of them.
2. Decide who will be the leader and who will be the timekeeper. Everyone else is a searcher!
3. Go outdoors and choose a finish line, where the timekeeper will be standing.
4. All the searchers close their eyes and stand facing a wall while the leader hides the objects.
5. When the leader says "PILOLO!"—which means "time to search for"—the searchers rush to find the hidden objects.
6. Whenever a hidden object is found, the searcher is given a point for bringing it to the finish line, where the timekeeper is.
7. The game ends when all the objects are found. The player who has found the most objects wins.

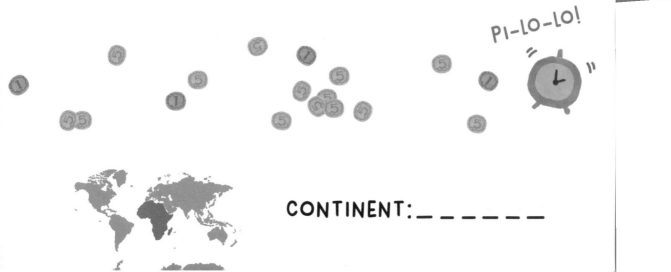

PI-LO-LO!

CONTINENT:_ _ _ _ _ _ _

I'm Akhilah from the Maldives!

IT'S QUIZ TIME

1. What is Maldives' official language?
   A. Tsonga
   B. Dhivehi

2. Many islands of the Maldives are threatened by ...
   A. Big sharks
   B. Rising sea levels

3. Maldivians used to build their houses using rocks from coral reefs. This is not allowed anymore because ...
   A. Coral reefs are protected
   B. Coral rock is too glittery and colorful

CAPITAL CITY: _ _ _ _

E L
M A

Let your imagination swim wild

Help Akilah and the fish design their underwater island, the Island of Hope.

WHAT YOU NEED:

- 1 large cereal box
- some colored cardstock
- scissors
- glue
- blue paint & paintbrush

YOU CAN ALSO USE:

- kinetic sand (or cheerios as sand)
- shells
- green pipe cleaners as seaweed
- googly eyes for the fishies

1. Cut out one of the two sides of your cereal box as shown.
2. Paint the inside of the box blue to make it look like the ocean.
3. Use different-colored cardstock to make fish. You can trace the fish below or you can make your own.
4. Decorate the Island of Hope in whichever way you like.

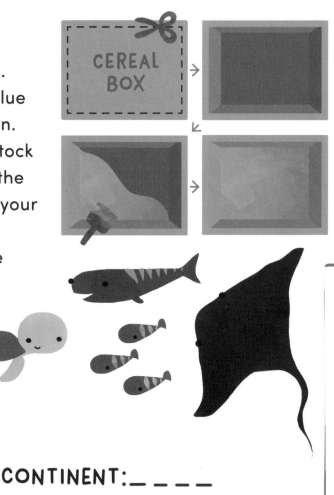

CONTINENT:_ _ _ _

I'm Suhail from India!

IT'S QUIZ TIME

1. Which sport is India famous for?

    A. Cricket

    B. Surfing

2. What were the Kings and Queens of India called?

    A. Shers and tandooris

    B. *Maharajas* and *maharanis*

3. What is the Taj Mahal?

A. India's famous mausoleum and one of the New Seven Wonders of the World

    B. India's most spicy dish

CAPITAL CITY: ___ _____

I D L
N W E
E H

Snakes & ladders

The famous game "snakes and ladders" was invented in India.
Shall we play? All you need is to find a buddy to play with,
two small objects that you can use as playing tokens and two dice.

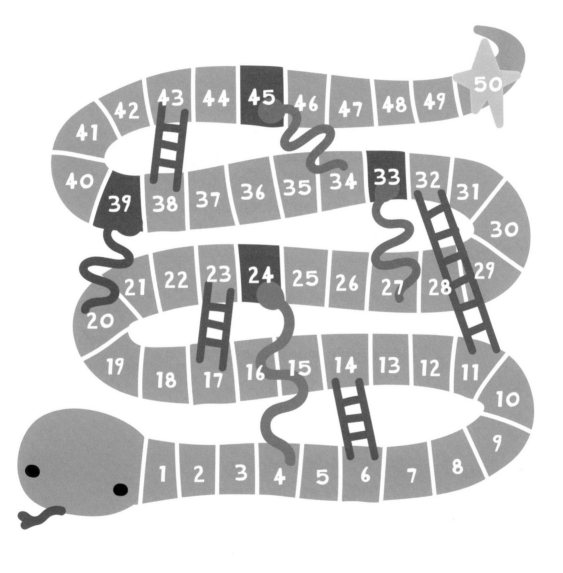

CONTINENT:_ _ _ _

I'm Charlotte from Canada!

IT'S QUIZ TIME

1. June 21 is Canada's National Indigenous Day. What is it?
   A. It's a day during which Canadians celebrate their Indigenous population, which were the first people to live there
   B. It's a day during which Canadians celebrate their diverse landscapes

2. Which of these animals live in Canada?
   A. Polar bears, narwhals and beavers
   B. Polar bears, penguins and beavers

3. The Inuit are one of Canada's Indigenous populations. What did they invent?
   A. Parkas and kayaks
   B. Maple syrup and canoes

CAPITAL CITY: _ _ _ _ _ _ _

T A T
O W A

How many jars?

Charlotte travels across Canada to give maple syrup to all her friends! Can you help her find out how many jars she'll need? Draw the correct number of maple syrup jars next to each animal.

BEAVER NEEDS ONE JAR,
AMKA NEEDS TWICE AS MANY AS BEAVER,
NARWHAL NEEDS TWICE AS MANY AS AMKA AND
POLAR BEAR NEEDS TWICE AS MANY AS NARWHAL.

CONTINENT:_ _ _ _ _ _
_ _ _ _ _ _ _

I'm Namelok from Kenya!

IT'S QUIZ TIME

1. Who are the Maasai?

A. One of the most famous tribes in Kenya, who are known for their local traditions and for leading a semi-nomadic life

B. The name given to all the important people of Kenya

2. With over 68 spoken languages, the official languages of Kenya are English and ...

A. Zulu

B. Swahili

3. Which of these animals can you find in Kenya?

A. Tigers, peacocks, orangutans, polar bears and penguins

B. Elephants, lions, cheetahs, giraffes, zebras, hippos and rhinos

CAPITAL CITY: _ _ _ _ _ _ _

R O
A I
N
I B

Have a movie night

But not just any movie. Choose a movie with a zebra!
Cuddle up with some pillows and your favorite snacks.

CONTINENT: _ _ _ _ _ _

I'm Zahara from Tanzania!

IT'S QUIZ TIME

1. Tanzanians often use the phrase
hakuna matata. What does it mean?

A. It means "no problem, everything is fine"
B. It means "the sun is shining"

2. What is the Great Migration
of animals?

A. An event during which about 2 million animals
move across Kenya and Tanzania in search
of grass
B. The time during which animals across Tanzania
give birth

3. What is Zanzibar?

A. A group of beautiful islands in Tanzania
with white, sandy beaches and coconut trees
B. A group of bars in Tanzania that serve
delicious juices and coconuts

CAPITAL CITY: _ _ _ _ _ _

D A D O O M

Climbing schedule

Mount Kilimanjaro in Tanzania is the tallest mountain in Africa. Thousands of people climb it every year. There are 70 people waiting to climb the mountain. Help Zahara create a schedule so that the visitors are equally distributed across the week.

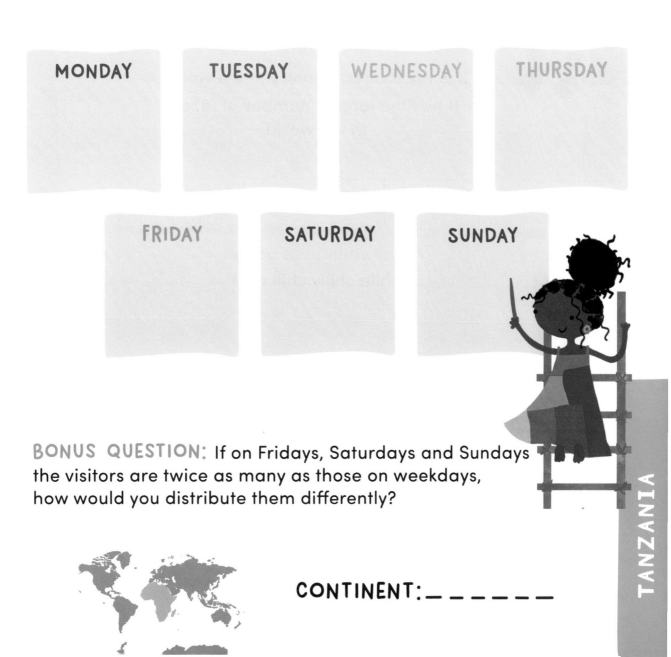

MONDAY	TUESDAY	WEDNESDAY	THURSDAY

FRIDAY	SATURDAY	SUNDAY

BONUS QUESTION: If on Fridays, Saturdays and Sundays the visitors are twice as many as those on weekdays, how would you distribute them differently?

TANZANIA

CONTINENT: _ _ _ _ _ _

I'm Alejandro from Chile!

IT'S QUIZ TIME

1. What is true about Chile?

A. It is the longest country in the world

B. It has the largest number of lakes in the world

2. Chile has a strong tradition of poetry. Because of this, it's sometimes called ...

A. The country of poets

B. Chile chilly chill chill

3. Chile has a delicious hot dog variation! What is it called?

A. *Completo*

B. Chill dog

CAPITAL CITY: _ _ _ _ _ _ _ _

T I A
N A O
S G

A poem for the ages

Chile is known as *país de poetas*, which means "country of poets". This is because it was home to some great poets, such as Nobel Prize winners Gabriela Mistral and Pablo Neruda. Let's wake up the little poet inside you! Write your own poem. Use any or all of the following words. Think of a story, a person, a place or a feeling that can be the inspiration of this poem—this can help with your writing. Your poem can rhyme, but it doesn't have to.

ABRACADABRA

SUNBEAM

MOUNTAINS

NEVER

CHATTERBOX

ENCHANTING

DELIGHTFUL

BUNNY

MUFFLED

DARK

CONTINENT: _ _ _ _ _ _

_ _ _ _ _ _ _

CHILE

I'm Marielle from France!

IT'S QUIZ TIME

1. Paris is known as the "City of Light" for many reasons. One reason is ...

A. Because in the 1600s, the King placed lanterns on the main streets and asked residents to light their windows to make Paris safer

B. Because in the 1600s, the King of France always wore yellow clothes and loved to sunbathe

2. The Louvre Museum is ...

A. The biggest art museum in the world

B. The second biggest art museum in the world

3. The Tour de France is a cycling race that takes place every summer. What does the person in the lead of the race wear at the end of each day?

A. Yellow undrewear

B. A yellow jersey

CAPITAL CITY: _ _ _ _ _   P   A   I
                                        S   R

Your grand idea

In the 1700s, during the Age of Enlightenment,
Paris became a center of flourishing ideas.
A lot of famous artists, poets, scientists
and philosophers lived there.

Pretend that you're also living in Paris during
that time! What would your grand idea be?
Spend the next week to work on your own
little project. Make, write, draw, perform
or discover anything you want.

Remember—the world needs your unique talents.
Work on them with all your heart, mind and soul.

CONTINENT:_ _ _ _ _ _ _

I'm Ivan from Russia!

IT'S QUIZ TIME

1. Russia is the largest country
in the world. It also has ...

A. The largest area of forests on the planet
B. The largest number of pools on the planet

2. What are *matryoshka* dolls?

A. A set of wooden, identical dolls of different
sizes, where one is placed inside the other
B. A set of five plastic dolls,
each portraying a different feeling

3. With over 100 thousand of them,
Russia has the biggest population of ...

A. Polar bears
B. Brown bears

CAPITAL CITY:_ _ _ _ _ _ _   M C W
                              O S O

Museum stroll

The State Hermitage Museum in Saint Petersburg is the biggest museum in the world. Museums are a wonderful place to spend an afternoon! You can wander around looking at paintings, pictures, sculptures and more. Visit a museum and choose a work of art that you like. Draw it below. Learn more about its backstory and the artist so that you can better understand how it came to life!

NAME OF PAINTING:
ARTIST:
MUSEUM:
WHY DID YOU LIKE IT?

CONTINENT:_ _ _ _ _ _ _
& _ _ _ _ _

I'm Karim from Egypt!

IT'S QUIZ TIME

1. Egypt is known for its pyramids.
Why were they initially built?

A. Most were built as tombs for the country's pharaohs

B. Each was built to welcome the arrival of a new member in the pharaohs' families

2. What are hieroglyphs?

A. The symbols and sketches Egyptians used to draw on pyramids

B. The writing system of Ancient Egypt that combined symbols, letters and syllables

3. The River Nile flows through Egypt and it's ...

A. The longest river in the world
B. A river with pink-colored water

CAPITAL CITY: _ _ _ _ _

I A O
R C

Build your own pyramid

Spend a whole day looking for pyramid-shaped objects.
Count them. How many can you find?

At the end of the day, make your own pyramid.
Find building blocks, matchboxes, shoe boxes,
pillows or anything else you can think of.
Start with a solid square base and build up to the top.

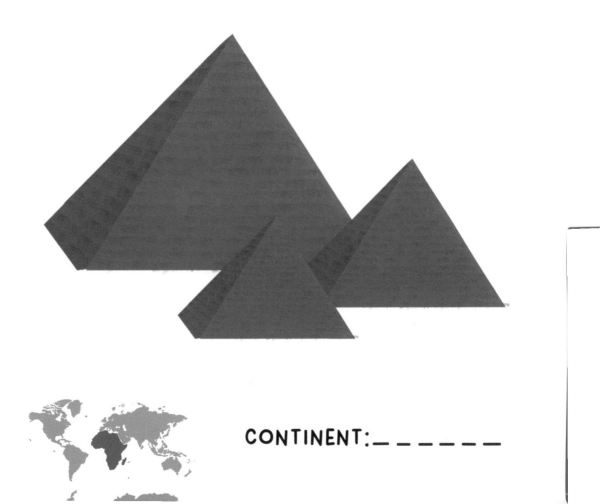

CONTINENT:_ _ _ _ _ _

I'm Millie from Australia!

IT'S QUIZ TIME

1. Which of these animals can only be found in Australia?

A. Kangaroos and koalas
B. Kangaroos and manatees

2. Next to Australia lies the largest coral system in the world. What is it called?

A. The Oceanic Blue Fishy Reef
B. The Great Barrier Reef

3. Who are the Anangu people?

A. The Aboriginal tribes of Australia
B. The people that live in the rural parts of Australia

CAPITAL CITY:_____   E R A N C B A R

Make fairy bread

Fairy bread is an old-fashioned Australian snack often made for birthday parties or for Australia Day—26 of January—which is the national day of Australia.

WHAT YOU NEED: • sliced bread • butter • sprinkles

1. Take slices of bread as they are, or cut them in fun shapes.
2. Spread butter on them. When the bread is slightly frozen, it's easier to spread the butter.
3. Add lots of sprinkles or, as the Australians call them, 100s and 1000s, over each slice.

BUDDIFUL FACT:

Fairy bread was a children's poem by Robert Louis Stevenson. Make sure to read it out loud while enjoying your sweet treat.

"Come up here, o dusty feet!
Here is fairy bread to eat.
Here in my retiring room,
Children, you may dine
On the golden smell of broom
And the shade of pine;
And when you have eaten well,
Fairy stories hear and tell. "

CONTINENT: _ _ _ _ _ _ _ _ _

I'm Ligia from Colombia!

IT'S QUIZ TIME

1. The phrase *quiubo* is used in Colombia very often. What does it mean?
   A. It means "wonderful"
   B. It means "what's up"

2. What is *ciclovía*?
   A. An event that happens in Bogotá every Sunday, during which cars are banned from the streets and the roads overflow with cyclists, roller skaters and strollers
   B. Bogotá's annual cycling competition

3. Guatapé in Colombia is ...
   A. A river that runs across the country
   B. The country's most colorful town

CAPITAL CITY: _ _ _ _ _ _ _

T O A
G B O O

Bicycles for all

Anyone can learn how to ride a bicycle, as long as they want and believe it. Can you design a special bike for each of the animals below?

CONTINENT: _ _ _ _ _ _
_ _ _ _ _ _ _

I'm Simo from Serbia!

IT'S QUIZ TIME

1. Serbia produces the largest amount of which fruit?

A. Bananas

B. Raspberries

2. Serbia is home to the beautiful Tara National Park. What activities can you do there?

A. Kayak, fishing, cycling and hiking

B. Horseback riding, ice hockey and wrestling

3. What is a *slava*?

A. A day to celebrate the Saint of each Serbian household, during which families gather with candles, red wine and cake

B. A day to celebrate the forests of Serbia, during which each family plants one tree in the wilderness

CAPITAL CITY:_ _ _ _ _ _ _ _

E G A
B R
D L E

Vampi, the pocket buddy

Have you ever wondered where vampire myths originated from?
That's right! Serbia! Our own Vampi is much friendlier, though.
He loves making new friends, going on adventures
and munching on raspberries—lots and lots of raspberries.
Create your own Vampi and carry him around with you.

WHAT YOU NEED: ● pink felt ● black sharpie ● cotton for stuffing
● sewing tools ● buttons

1. Copy Vampi's design on felt using a black sharpie. Repeat it once.
2. Cut out the two Vampi designs.
3. Call a grownup to join the fun.
4. Place cotton in between the two felt pieces and with the help of a grownup, sew them together.
5. Attach buttons to give Vampi eyes.
6. Use the sharpie to draw his mouth.
7. Put Vampi in your pocket and take him everywhere with you. Don't forget to get some raspberries to feed him whenever he's hungry.

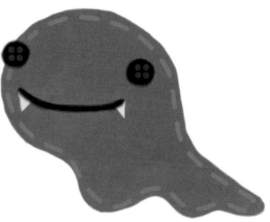

BUDDIFUL TIP: Hard to find some of the material listed above?
You can always improvise!

CONTINENT:_ _ _ _ _ _ _

I'm Adri from Mexico!

IT'S QUIZ TIME

1. Mexico is home to many pyramids. The most famous one is also one of the New Seven Wonders of the World and it's called ...
   A. Chichén Itzá
   B. Machu Picchu

2. What is a *sombrero*?
   A. A Mexican hat that is large and round
   B. The way Mexicans refer to a guitar

3. What is *Dia de los Muertos*, which means "the Day of the Dead"?
   A. A Mexican holiday to remember all the loved ones who have passed away
   B. The way Mexicans refer to a funeral

CAPITAL CITY: _ _ _ _ _ _ _ _ _ _

C M T I O
E X Y C I

Let's make alebrijes

Alebrijes are colorful mythical creatures that combine features of various animals. Copy the designs below—with or without using tracing paper. Use the base of an axolotl—a Mexican salamander—and give it wings, horns, funny ears and anything else you like! Color it with different patterns or even create your own alebrijes.

CONTINENT:_ _ _ _ _ _

_ _ _ _ _ _ _ _

I'm Ella from Denmark!

IT'S QUIZ TIME

1. Which famous storyteller is from Denmark?
    A. The brothers Grimm
    B. Hans Christian Andersen

2. Which is the oldest amusement park
in the world that can be found in Denmark?
    A. Tivoli
    B. Bakken

3. Who were the Vikings?
    A. They were Scandinavian explorers, traders
and warriors that traveled across Europe
    B. They were the Danish crop growers,
famous for cultivating corn and beans

CAPITAL CITY:_ _ _ _ _ _ _ _ _ _

O G C N H
P
N E A E

Become a storyteller

"Thumbelina", "The Little Mermaid" and "The Princess and the Pea" are some of the most famous children's stories written in Denmark. Use inspiration from these stories and become a storyteller. The story can start like this:

ONCE UPON A TIME, A LITTLE MERMAID FOUND A TINY GIRL SITTING ON A WATERLILY IN THE MIDDLE OF A POND. "COME CLOSER," THE TINY GIRL SAID TO THE MERMAID AND OPENED HER PALM. SHE WAS HOLDING A PEA.

CONTINENT:_ _ _ _ _ _

I'm Marcia from Jamaica!

IT'S QUIZ TIME

1. What is Jamaican Patois?

A. It's Jamaica's national anthem—
a combination of reggae music and poetry

B. It's Jamaica's slang language—
a combination of English and words from West Africa

2. Which of the following is Jamaica's national dish?

A. Cod and chips

B. Ackee and saltfish

3. Who was Bob Marley?

A. Jamaica's first president who named the country Xaymaca, which means "land of springs"

B. A famous Jamaican singer and songwriter, as well as a pioneer of reggae music

CAPITAL CITY:_ _ _ _ _ _ _ _

TOKINGSN

Jamaica geometry jam

Marcia and her friends discovered a secret passage behind
Dunn's River Falls that leads to the world's longest rainbow.
Along the passage, there are rocks of different shapes.
Can you count them? You can also color them in
with their respective color!

■ ... SQUARES		▢ ... RECTANGLES	
▲ ... TRIANGLES		◆ ... RHOMBUSES	
● ... CIRCLES		▰ ... TRAPEZOIDS	

CONTINENT:_ _ _ _ _ _
_ _ _ _ _ _ _

I'm Hiba from Syria!

IT'S QUIZ TIME

1. What is a *souq*?

A. An open-air marketplace usually divided into narrows streets with different sections

B. A closed-air marketplace in which people take cover during the winter months

2. Which of these is a yummy Syrian dessert?

A. *Kanafeh*—it's made of filo pastry and cheese

B. *Mille-feuille*—it's made of delicious layers of puff pastry and cream

3. What is special about the Arabic language?

A. In the Arabic language sentences can only have five words

B. In the Arabic language you read and write from right to left

CAPITAL CITY:_ _ _ _ _ _ _ _

D M C
A U
A S S

Souq adventures

Hiba is shopping for spices in the *souqs*. Help her choose the correct path to arrive at the stand with the spices. Color it in!

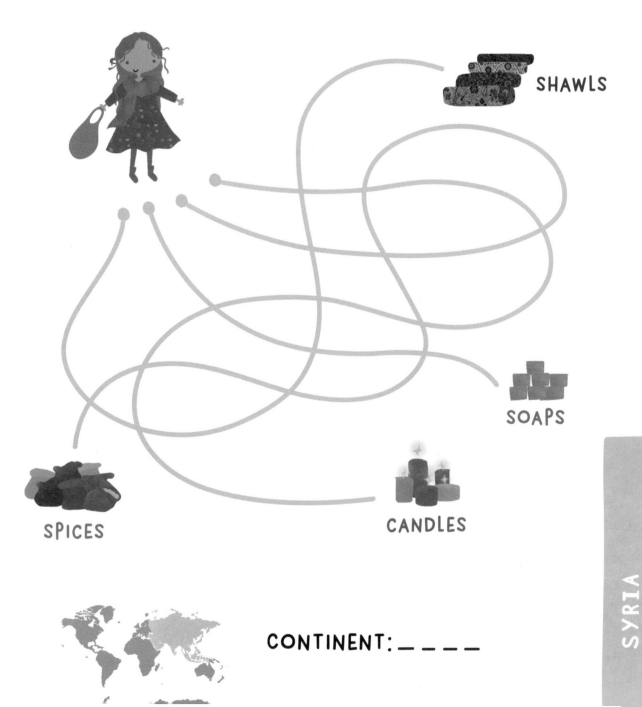

SHAWLS

SOAPS

SPICES

CANDLES

CONTINENT: _ _ _ _

I'm Mei Ling from China!

IT'S QUIZ TIME

1. A tangram is ...

A. A seven-piece geometric puzzle

B. A dragon that is famous across China

2. Chinese New Year is celebrated on ...

A. The 1st of January

B. A different day every year, some time between January and February

3. Which of the following symbols represent good luck in China?

A. Eagles, the number 2237, chopsticks, butterflies

B. Dragons, the color red, sky lanterns, crickets

CAPITAL CITY: _ _ _ _ _ _ _

I B
N J G I
E

China's furry friends

Name each animal and match the words below
with their description.

SEAL   MONKEY   BAMBOO   PINK

PANDA   DOLPHIN   ICE   TREES

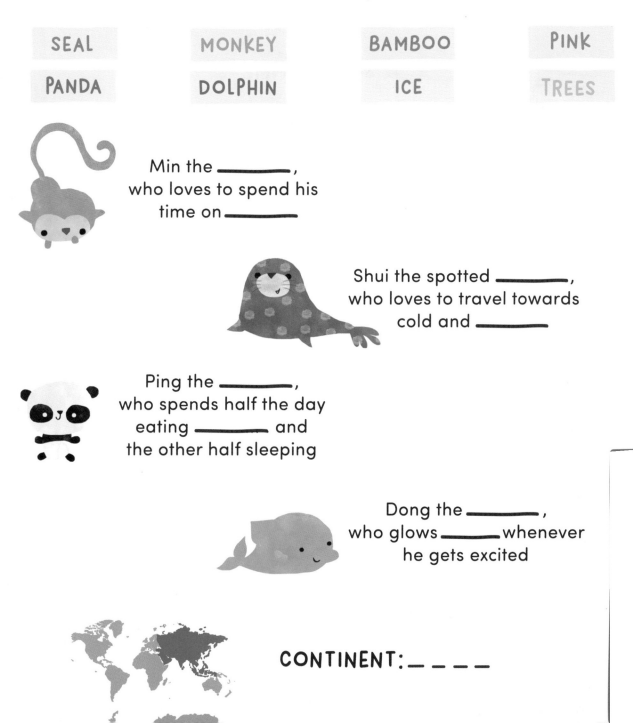

Min the _____,
who loves to spend his
time on _____

Shui the spotted _____,
who loves to travel towards
cold and _____

Ping the _____,
who spends half the day
eating _____ and
the other half sleeping

Dong the _____,
who glows _____ whenever
he gets excited

CONTINENT: _ _ _ _

I'm Manaia from New Zealand!

IT'S QUIZ TIME

1. Why are New Zealanders often referred to as "kiwis"?

A. Because they eat a lot of kiwi fruit

B. Because the national animal of New Zealand is the kiwi, a fluffy flightless bird

2. Which are the three official languages of New Zealand?

A. English, Māori and Tanganese

B. English, Māori and the New Zealand Sign Language

3. Who were the first people to live in New Zealand?

A. The Māori

B. The Paua

CAPITAL CITY: _ _ _ _ _ _ _ _ _ _

N E N I T W
L G L O

Sheep sheep sheep

New Zealand has over 25 million sheep—that's A LOT of sheep, don't you think? Make some sheep figurines to accompany you throughout your day.

WHAT YOU NEED:
- glue • scissors • a piece of paper • cotton balls
- sticks or matches • neutral & dark-colored cardstock

1. Take a piece of paper and roll it into a ball.
2. Take cotton balls and stick them around the piece of paper to make your sheep extra fluffy.
3. Use cardstock to cut out the head, eyes and ears.
4. Use four sticks (or matches) for the legs.

BAAA

MAKE A WHOLE FLOCK OF THEM!

CONTINENT:_ _ _ _ _ _ _ _

I'm Katrina from the Philippines!

IT'S QUIZ TIME

1. Each Filipino province has its own festival. They are grand, vibrant and full of color! What are they known for?

A. It's a chance for Filipinos to exhibit their rich culture and honor their history and patron saints

B. They attract tourists and show them the steps to all their different dances

2. What are *Jeepneys*?

A. They are old Jeeps that are decorated with colorful patterns and serve as buses in the Philippines

B. They are old Jeeps that can be found at the entrance of every Filipino museum

3. Tarsiers can be found in the forests of the Philippines. What do they look like?

A. They have big eyes and a round head that rotates 180°

B. They have tiny eyes and a round head that rotates 180°

CAPITAL CITY: _ _ _ _ _ _ _

L
N A A
  I M

Tarsier puppet forest

Make your own tarsier finger puppets and bring them to life. Give them their own character, make up your own stories and act them out using the puppets by making distinct, funny voices.

1. Trace the puppets on paper. *

2. Color them in and cut them out.

3. Wrap the sides of each tarsier around your finger and secure them with tape.

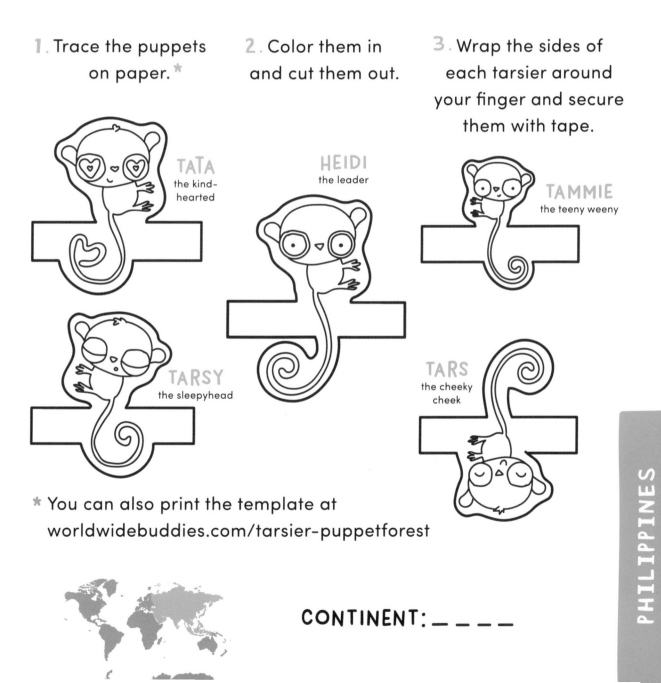

TATA
the kind-hearted

HEIDI
the leader

TAMMIE
the teeny weeny

TARSY
the sleepyhead

TARS
the cheeky cheek

* You can also print the template at
worldwidebuddies.com/tarsier-puppetforest

CONTINENT: _ _ _ _

PHILIPPINES

I'm Henry from the United States!

IT'S QUIZ TIME

1. The first man to walk on the Moon was American. His name was ...
- **A.** Arthur Miller
- **B.** Neil Armstrong

2. Which of these sports started in the USA?
- **A.** Cricket and skiing
- **B.** Baseball and basketball

3. What is the Thanksgiving holiday?
- **A.** A holiday during which families come together to be thankful for the harvest
- **B.** A holiday during which families come together to celebrate their children

CAPITAL CITY: _ _ _ _ _ _ _ _ _ _

W H N I T N A S G O

50 states of mind

The United States of America has 50 different states and ...
it's time to memorize them! Read the list below and say it out loud
a few—or more—times. Then, start trying to memorize them
in alphabetical order. Have fun!

1. ALABAMA
2. ALASKA
3. ARIZONA
4. ARKANSAS
5. CALIFORNIA
6. COLORADO
7. CONNECTICUT
8. DELAWARE
9. FLORIDA
10. GEORGIA
11. HAWAII
12. IDAHO
13. ILLINOIS

14. INDIANA
15. IOWA
16. KANSAS
17. KENTUCKY
18. LOUISIANA
19. MAINE
20. MARYLAND
21. MASSACHUSETTS
22. MICHIGAN
23. MINNESOTA
24. MISSISSIPPI
25. MISSOURI
26. MONTANA

27. NEBRASKA
28. NEVADA
29. NEW HAMPSHIRE
30. NEW JERSEY
31. NEW MEXICO
32. NEW YORK
33. NORTH CAROLINA
34. NORTH DAKOTA
35. OHIO
36. OKLAHOMA
37. OREGON
38. PENNSYLVANIA
39. RHODE ISLAND

40. SOUTH CAROLINA
41. SOUTH DAKOTA
42. TENNESSEE
43. TEXAS
44. UTAH
45. VERMONT
46. VIRGINIA
47. WASHINGTON
48. WEST VIRGINIA
49. WISCONSIN
50. WYOMING

BUDDIFUL TIP: Remember the number you should be at
whenever a new letter starts to make sure you're on the right path.
For example, after you've recalled 18 states, you should be at the
letter "M".

CONTINENT:_ _ _ _ _

_ _ _ _ _ _ _

And we're Eli & Nelly from Cyprus!

IT'S QUIZ TIME

1. What is a *lefkaritiko*?

A. The way people greet each other
in the Cypriot village of Pano Lefkara

B. A handmade lace with intricate geometric patterns
made in the Cypriot village of Pano Lefkara

2. What is Petra tou Romiou known for?

A. It's the birthplace of Aphrodite,
Goddess of Beauty and Love

B. It's a big rock in the middle of the ocean
and the home of 53 aliens

3. What is *shoushoukos*?

A. A meeting place where Cypriots gather to drink coffee,
play backgammon and converse with each other

B. A chewy sweet made with a mixture of grape juice,
flour and nuts

CAPITAL CITY: _ _ _ _ _ _ _ _

I S
I
N C
O A

The ocean's clue

Cyprus emerged from the sea over a million years ago. And you can still spot some traces of it. Connect the dots in the image below to unravel the clue that can be found at Troodos mountain.

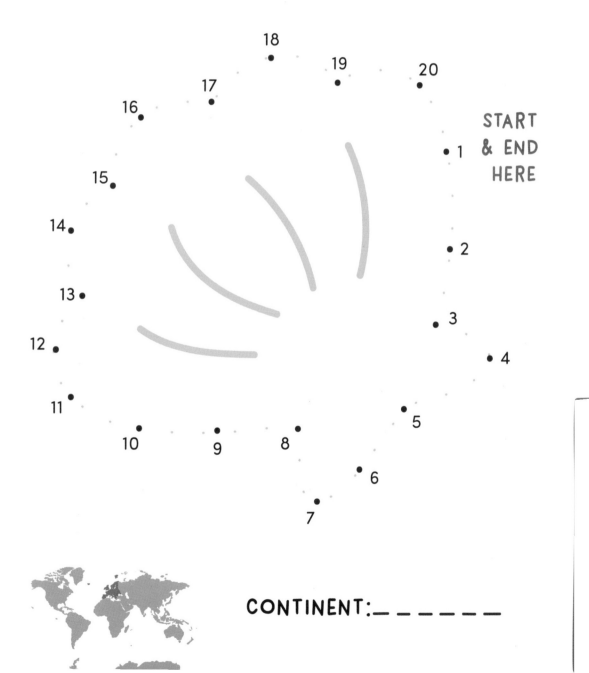

18
19
20
17
16
START
& END
HERE
• 1
15
14
• 2
13
• 3
12
• 4
11
5
10
9
8
6
7

CONTINENT:_ _ _ _ _ _

QUIZ ANSWERS

PERU	South America, Lima	Quiz: 1B, 2A, 3B
GREECE	Europe, Athens	Quiz: 1A, 2B, 3B
BRAZIL	South America, Brasília	Quiz: 1B, 2A, 3A
NIGERIA	Africa, Abuja	Quiz: 1B, 2B, 3A
THE NETHERLANDS	Europe, Amsterdam	Quiz: 1A, 2A, 3B
IRAN	Asia, Tehran	Quiz: 1A, 2A, 3A
SOUTH AFRICA	Africa, Cape Town (1 of 3)	Quiz: 1B, 2B, 3A
JAPAN	Asia, Tokyo	Quiz: 1B, 2A, 3A
GHANA	Africa, Accra	Quiz: 1B, 2A, 3A
MALDIVES	Asia, Malé	Quiz: 1B, 2B, 3A
INDIA	Asia, New Delhi	Quiz: 1A, 2B, 3A
CANADA	North America, Ottawa	Quiz: 1A, 2A, 3A
KENYA	Africa, Nairobi	Quiz: 1A, 2B, 3B
TANZANIA	Africa, Dodoma	Quiz: 1A, 2A, 3A
CHILE	South America, Santiago	Quiz: 1A, 2A, 3A
FRANCE	Europe, Paris	Quiz: 1A, 2B, 3B
RUSSIA	Europe & Asia, Moscow	Quiz: 1A, 2A, 3B
EGYPT	Africa, Cairo	Quiz: 1A, 2B, 3A
AUSTRALIA	Oceania, Canberra	Quiz: 1A, 2B, 3A
COLOMBIA	South America, Bogotá	Quiz: 1B, 2A, 3B
SERBIA	Europe, Belgrade	Quiz: 1B, 2A, 3A
MEXICO	North America, Mexico City	Quiz: 1A, 2A, 3A
DENMARK	Europe, Copenhagen	Quiz: 1B, 2B, 3A
JAMAICA	North America, Kingston	Quiz: 1B, 2B, 3B
SYRIA	Asia, Damascus	Quiz: 1A, 2A, 3B
CHINA	Asia, Beijing	Quiz: 1A, 2B, 3B
NEW ZEALAND	Oceania, Wellington	Quiz: 1B, 2B, 3A
PHILIPPINES	Asia, Manila	Quiz: 1A, 2A, 3A
USA	North America, Washington	Quiz: 1B, 2B, 3A
CYPRUS	Europe, Nicosia	Quiz: 1B, 2A, 3B

MY ACTIVITY CHECKLIST

- ◯ A SALTY ICE CHALLENGE
- ◯ CROSSWORD MYTHS
- ◯ THE AMAZON RAINFOREST
- ◯ KINDNESS CHALLENGES
- ◯ A TULIPFUL PATTERN
- ◯ SPROUTS 101
- ◯ WILDERNESS WORD TRAIL
- ◯ ORIGAMI SECRETS
- ◯ PI-LO-LO FUN
- ◯ LET YOUR IMAGINATION SWIM WILD
- ◯ SNAKES & LADDERS
- ◯ HOW MANY JARS?
- ◯ HAVE A MOVIE NIGHT
- ◯ CLIMBING SCHEDULE
- ◯ A POEM FOR THE AGES

- ◯ YOUR GRAND IDEA
- ◯ MUSEUM STROLL
- ◯ BUILD YOUR OWN PYRAMID
- ◯ FAIRY BREAD
- ◯ BICYCLES FOR ALL
- ◯ VAMPI, THE POCKET BUDDY
- ◯ LET'S MAKE ALEBRIJES
- ◯ BECOME A STORYTELLER
- ◯ JAMAICA GEOMETRY JAM
- ◯ SOUQ ADVENTURES
- ◯ CHINA'S FURRY FRIENDS
- ◯ SHEEP SHEEP SHEEP
- ◯ TARSIER PUPPET FOREST
- ◯ 50 STATES OF MIND
- ◯ THE OCEAN'S CLUE

ACTIVITY ANSWERS

CROSSWORD MYTHS: 1. Music, 2. Twelve, 3. Foam, 4. Mythology, 5. Zeus

THE AMAZON RAINFOREST: Emergent (birds, butterflies), Canopy (monkey, toucans, iguanas, sloths), Understory (snakes, jaguars), Forest floor (insects, frogs, ant-eaters, jaguars)

HOW MANY JARS? Amka – 2, Narwhal – 4, Polar Bear – 8

CLIMBING SCHEDULE: 10 each day, BONUS: 7 on Mondays, Tuesdays, Wednesdays, Thursdays & 14 on Fridays, Saturdays and Sundays

JAMAICA GEOMETRY JAM: 5 squares, 9 circles, 7 rhombuses, 8 triangles, 4 rectangles, 3 trapezoids

CHINA'S FURRY FRIENDS: Min the monkey – time on trees, Shui the spotted seal- cold and ice, Ping the panda - eating bamboo, Dong the dolphin - glows pink

COMPLETE YOUR COLLECTION, MEET ALL OUR BUDDIES AND EXPLORE THE WORLD!

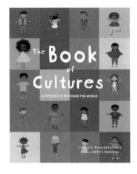

WORLDWIDE
BUDDIES

At Worldwide Buddies, we have created a universe of buddies from different parts of the planet, specially designed for littles to embrace diverse perspectives. Our books and toys take readers on adventures near and far, encouraging them to explore our wonderful world.
Are you ready? Off we go!

LET'S BE BUDDIES!
FOLLOW US / TAG US @WORLDWIDEBUDDIES
WWW.WORLDWIDEBUDDIES.COM

PSST... LET'S GO ON A HUNT! HOW MANY MUSICAL INSTRUMENTS CAN YOU SPOT IN THIS ACTIVITY BOOK?

Around the World Activity Book
Printed in China, first print, 2023